THAT OLD-TIME RELIGION

Peter Didsbury was born in 1946 in Fleetwood, Lancashire, and moved to Hull at the age of six. After reading English and Hebrew at Oxford, he worked at various casual jobs, and later taught English at a large Hull comprehensive for eight years. He then completed an M. Phil. thesis, and now works as an archaeologist for Humberside County Council. He lives in Hull.

His poetry was featured prominently in Douglas Dunn's Hull anthology, *A Rumoured City* (Bloodaxe Books, 1982), and later in *The New Poetry* (Bloodaxe Books, 1993). He has published three collections with Bloodaxe, *The Butchers of Hull* (1982), *The Classical Farm* (1987) and *That Old-Time Religion* (1994). His last two collections have been Poetry Book Society Recommendations, and he won a Cholmondeley Award for *The Classical Farm*.

PETER DIDSBURY

✹

THAT
OLD-TIME
RELIGION

BLOODAXE BOOKS

ISBN: 1 85224 255 8

First published 1994 by
Bloodaxe Books Ltd,
P.O. Box 1SN,
Newcastle upon Tyne NE99 1SN.

Bloodaxe Books Ltd acknowledges
the financial assistance of Northern Arts.

For Edith Didsbury

Cover printing by J. Thomson Colour Printers Ltd, Glasgow.

Printed in Great Britain by
Bell & Bain Limited, Glasgow, Scotland.

Things we make up out of language turn into common property
ROY FISHER

Still, individual culture is also something
ARTHUR HUGH CLOUGH

Acknowledgements

Acknowledgements are due to the editors of the following publications in which some of these poems first appeared: *Bête Noire*, *The Chiron Review*, *The Jacaranda Review*, *The New Poetry* (Bloodaxe Books, 1993), *Poetry and Audience*, *Poetry Book Society Anthology 3* (PBS/Hutchinson, 1992), *Poetry with an Edge* (Bloodaxe Books, new edition, 1993), *The Times Literary Supplement*, *Verse* and *The Wide Skirt*.

Five of these poems were first published as *Common Property*, a limited edition pamphlet by Carnivorous Arpeggio 1992.

Contents

The Shore

A minute past noon,
and deeply cold on the shore.
The sun with its rare but un-marvellous halo
starts climbing back down the sky.
The air stills. Wind lies over field
like a razor held above a leather strop.
The beach is locked and hard.
Its uncut gems, and small round leaves
like patinated coins,
it keeps beneath plate glass.
How empty things are.
The cliff behind us acts from some notion of presence,
but very faintly, like a host of spirits
crowding to sip at a pool.
The world of phenomena gathers at the surface
of a system of unity powered by emptiness.
Hills. River. Line of winter farms.
A barge coming down the navigable channel
from somewhere inland, with nothing in its hold.

Passing the Park

(for Genny Rahtz)

I drive by the park
on a bright mid-winter morning.
It's just before lunch,
the car is falling to bits.
Trees conceal
a lake with water-birds.
There issue the sounds
of its undivided nature.
For once, it seems,
there is nothing at all to decide.
A simple song of impoverishment
is streaming like warmth
from the surface of the planet.
Up on the roof of the lodge by the gate
the cups of an anemometer
are turning round in the wind.

The Old Masters

Our lives are short,
and those who taught us have died.
They have taken into Sheol
their facial tics and their jokes.
Their nicknames now
are breathed beneath the ground,
with their black gowns flying
they stalk the touchlines of Hell.
Who pulls down on the brim of his cap
to such as these ones now?
Or who calls their names,
at the going down of the day?
They are come to nothing,
these mighty men of old,
are as air between goalposts
or chalk in the cracks of the floor.
For their classrooms know them not,
and neither are their voices heard in the Hall.
From *Big Field*, *Majuba* and *Spionkop*
their cries have long been carried by the wind.
They have all gone home,
and all the desks which remembered them are burned.
They have bent to their bike-clips at a quarter past four
and left the bike-sheds emptied of their bikes.
Their names are gone up in smoke.
Their insignia have vanished.
The teeth of them have been loosened on their pipes
and all their briefcases finally come unstitched.
Their day is over.
Their sum works out at nought.
From morning's blackboard the evening has erased
their map of the world, their scribbled declension of *ego*.
They have gone down into the grave-mouth and taken
their wartime ranks and all their fountain pens.
And now there are none alive which are like them.
And only their mark-books remain.

A Troubadour

O my lady, your delectable bottom,
pressed to the window-glass in the ancient tower,
defies the Heavens, and makes counterfeit the Moon.
Have mercy on your serving-man, my Lady,
if only for this, that in inventing you
your heretic may have grievous need of your boon.

Winter Quarters
(for Bryan Sitch)

I watched my letter go. Until that man
got lost inside the glen I held my breath.
When heads on poles above the double gates
all sighed at once, 'Oh heads,' I thought,
'I had not known you were friends.'

Then down from the wind. The thing was done.
My three good names in gracile coal-black hand
were gone from me, were going through slanting rain.
Each step I took across the levelled ground
was matched by one that bore my soul away.

In my room I ordered fire. At my command
a servant tended winter's blackened stones.
Then all night long I watched the flames aspire.
In wooden walls, to sit and watch wood burn,
was all Love wanted, all it knew of home.

Part of the Bridge

(for Robin Moore)

The enormous mentality
of the south bank abutment's
embedded concrete block
is not impassive,
though it copes with the westering sun
as remorselessly as any god with petitions.

It is not to be blamed for its size,
its faces textured with jutting tablets, grooves,
or even our dear conviction that mass,
when sheer enough, moves over into sentience.

To enter its zone on an evening in July
is to speak the word *temple*
in as emptiness-sanctioned a voice
as is used among the mountains;

to hear what it does with the fabulations of air,
that move in its precinct like spirits of ancient birds,
is to know both the paradox, and the stimulus, of its pity.

At North Villa

Flakes of white ash.
Then a telegram about them.

No such thing any more.
Good reason to make this "historical".

Such a message in 1902, then,
being read by a person standing at a window,
a mature person of sober religion and tastes.

It was the middle of that morning.
Wet gusts of wind were engaged in tearing
blossom from trees in his kerchief-sized orchard.
Somewhere deep in the house
a domestic servant was singing *con gusto*
her polystanzaic ballades.

Four posts a day in 1902
plus special delivery of parcels and telegrams.

To 'flakes of white ash' he decided he would reply
with 'a bushel of garden loam',
but could not imagine to whom
this would seem the appropriate courtesy.
An answer had almost suggested itself
when terrific commotion in process of being let loose
directly outside his room
made him open his door to find that *somehow or other*
a large wet dog had entered from the street
and was gaily disturbing with its wagging extremity
the contents of the hall umbrella stand.

The sound of iron-shod sticks being thus re-arranged
within the stand's rectangular tin tray
was a tympany he perceived he could do without.
Water shaken from the layered capes
of his housekeeper's shoulder, as she pirouetted and shooed,
determined him likewise to enter his study again.
His cabinet. The word had very power to soothe him,

and considering this he wiped his aids to vision
while taking the first of the dozen myopic steps
which would bring him back to his table,
a handsome affair of mahogany and leather
which being arrived at he returned his lamps to his nose
and bent to retrieve the missive concerning white ash.

He closed his eyes. He breathed out slowly.
He opened his eyes. And then he stooped again.
Failing to find it where memory told him it lay,
on the blotter, he searched with mounting frustration
the carpet, the mantelpiece, the window seat,
and behind the ormolu statuette of Anubis.
Being the kind of fellow he was
the relocation of that mislaid piece of intelligence
could have swelled in import till it engendered the undesirable,
but as it happened it was scarcely more than an hour
before his hand encountered, in that portion of his jacket
to which he had lately returned his Irish lawn,
a crumpled and now quite sodden piece of paper
which had clearly seen service between someone's finger and thumb.
Sighs fought with smiles, then, awarding his normally gathered
          countenance
a certain vigour, a wind in the unmown grass of a modest orchard,
a *canzone* defying an established compendage of doors.

He sat down.
Restoring the wire as best he could to its shape
he recalled how washing and shaving with the dawn
he'd looked forward to nothing more than a day with his coins.
But now all this.
Apple blossom pasted to the glass,
a mysterious telegram,
the speed with which he had not reached
an ungainsayable answer,
the wet black dog in his hall.

It was almost as if the house had decided
no longer to do without him, and to command his attention
was plucking his sleeve with what fingers it could form
from the strangeness of days and its own intelligence.
He did not feel afraid, he thought, then at once felt afraid

that the notion had entered his head. Who could tell now
what the rest of the daylight might hold?
Or by nightfall be lying
beneath his diarist's hand? Not *he*, he knew,
and began to rise by instinct from his chair,
who had dwelled in North Villa for nigh on forty years,
a second before he would hear the luncheon bell sound.

An Egregious Talent

Arse-ripping farts were his speciality,
with which he would signal surprise, enquiry,
distaste, *ennui*, and contempt
with equal facility.

He did not suffer fools gladly,
and the condescending HARRUMPH
with which he was used to greet imbecility
made him feared throughout Europe, in his time, apparently.

A Moment's Reflection

The books, the booze,
the more than a third
of a million cigarettes.

The terrible need to enthuse.

If you'd not been yourself
you might have kept pets,
but you are, haven't you heard?

It's not as if life were stored on a shelf
and all you had to do was reach down
some walls of pale blue plaster,
a plump satin heart, a piece of alabaster.

You're not around to choose.

You'd hardly be sitting here
costing the vital parts
of this most costly of all arts
if you'd had a say in the matter, now would you?

The Gun

(for Lex Barker)

I found a gun in a field, barrel burst,
stock rotted away. I took it home
and removed the worst of the rust with a brush,
standing at night on the kitchen doorstep.
I used to dream about guns,
while sleeping I mean,
but gradually that stopped happening to me.
I don't know why I brought it home that day,
I suppose it seemed not *any* piece of scrap,
but all it does is lie by the back door,
unremarked by all who come to the house.
No one seems to notice this old gun,
but if I tell them its story they all act the same,
must see it, hold it, express delight at my luck.
In some odd way the thing has become a touchstone,
though of what is proving difficult to tell.
I suspect it has helped me to love my friends
more nearly than before, if that were possible,
for I've shewn it to several now, and so far none of them
has failed to wonder if it might have murdered someone.

The Shorter 'Life'

I loved the rain,
but always suffered badly
from post-pluvial *tristesse*.

My best wet afternoon was in the mouth
of a disused railway tunnel,
behind me the mile-long carbon-encrusted dark.

That Old-Time Religion

(for Gordon Ostler)

God and His angels stroll in the garden
before turning in for the night.
They've adopted the style
of rich and gifted young Englishmen this evening
and also, bizarrely even for them, decided that they'll speak
in nothing but Sumerian to each other
which all are agreed was a truly heavenly language.

It isn't long before God starts boasting,
in Sumerian of course, that He's the only Being He knows
Who knows by heart *The Bothie of Tober-na-Vuolich*,
and is about to prove it when Lucifer intercedes
to make the points that

   a) they've all agreed to speak Sumerian, which was never the
      tongue of that estimable poem, and that unless He wants to
      pay the usual forfeit, which wouldn't really be consonant
      with His divinity, He'd better give up the idea;

   b) should He decide to do it into
      instantaneous and perfect Sumerian metres,
      a feat of which they're all aware He's capable,
      He wouldn't be proving His grasp of the original
      and would run the risk of them thinking Him a show-off;

& c) since He, God, and not Arthur Hugh Clough must be regarded
     as the only true author of *The Bothie*, as of all things,
     he, Satan, doesn't see what the point of it would be anyway.

In the silence which follows the Creator is keenly aware
of the voice of the nightingale, then murmurs of consensus,
then much delighted laughter from the angels.

Lucifer bows.

The nightingale stops singing.

God sighs. He could really do without these bitches sometimes
but *then* where would He be?

As if to answer this question to Himself
He withdraws to the farthest reaches of the garden
and leans on the parapet, smoking in fitful gloom,
for what seems like an eternity.
He lights each gasper from the butt of His last
then flicks the glowing end far into the dark,
displeased at His foreknowledge of where it will fall.
To KNOW what His more intelligent creatures have thought
of these lights that appear in August out of Perseus
and not to have disabused them of it, as He's always meant to,
is unforgivable. He gazes in their direction in the dark
and gives them His Word that soon He will change all that,
silent at first, then whispered, then *shouted* in Sumerian.

In a Gothic Yard

(for George Messo)

The tables here are the upturned hooves
of ruined equestrian statues.

The floor is unraked sand,
the service nothing to speak of.

We wait for our foaming maplewood bowls
(of mare's milk, sometimes blood)
and pass an hour attempting to bring to mind,
out of courteous silence,
the plashing of civic fountains.

Knowing that a fountain was not a god,
or a sign denoting a brothel,
has become a badge of learning,
a certain distinction of class.

The foolish and unkempt are coming to think
of bronze as a kind of stone,
pour drinks for horsemen inverted under the ground.

At Her Grinding-Stone

Something about the land.
As if it had taken her elbow, aside,
to tell her an unwanted secret.
The land itself. The sun's high
wheel at noon–tide,
the rutted lane behind the circular houses,
as if the next lot's god had been spotted
sleeping drunk beneath a hedge,
that kind of time-wasting rumour.

Something to do with her worth.
As if all ways of being wife or daughter,
now and forever, had been dreamed at the edge of a field.
Her grinding-stone. Her going down
to the spring-fed pools in the mire,
the stones of her hearth, her raftered pharmacopoeia,
as if the woods had sidled close together
to pronounce her name with another's, most shaming whisper,
most insolent rumour of all.

Words for a Sundial

Approach not me,
but enquire instead
of the great god Fuck,
who almost certainly knows.

Topographical Note

The farmhouses here have no front doors,
just collections of side and back entrances.
They're surrounded by unkempt hedges alive with birds,
and their tenants sit in parlours deep inside them
and stare at walls hung with paintings of fishes and fruit.

In My Kitchen

Boots on last week's newspaper,
flakes of mud on the floor

First to look into freshly opened tomb,
at withered garlands,
plaster fallen from ceiling

Only known as pictograms till now
in texts to do with dusk

But now we have seen the real thing
and how black they are
and how much like our own boots

A Letter to an Editor

(for John Osborne)

Dear Sir
thank you for your letter
asking for some poems
and offering to pay me for them
but I haven't got any left.

I could really have done with
a cheque for £42
but there it is.

I've been working on one
about a hare breaking out
from a square of long grass
beneath an electricity pylon
then vanishing like cold light
across a level arable field
but it isn't finished yet
so I hardly feel that I'm in a position
to be able to let you see it.

I've got it to the point now
where I'm totally clear in my mind
about how that kind of event
is characterised by its emptiness,
gains birth in the void etcetera,
but can't yet resolve in formal terms the equation
between the ogre-bestridden farm in question
and dark wet nights of the kind on which
it forcibly enters my head.

Alas. With 38 quid I could have added to my library
of monographs on Roman pottery
of the first to fourth century,
the structured retrieval of which from the ploughsoil
was my only reason for being
in the middle of that field in the first place.

Still. There we have it.

It occurs to me, by the way, and if it's any help,
that should my inability to deliver the goods on this occasion
seriously inconvenience your 'Margoulis K. Grolsz issue' plans
then a dozen punctuation marks and a few bright nouns
aspersed on an otherwise utterly blank white page
with my name at the top of it
would probably go unquestioned by your readers
and a very long way toward solving both our problems.
We might thus bring down two birds with one handful of gravel
and payment on a *pro rata* basis would of course be acceptable.

You will be aware, I feel sure, that my friendship with Grolsz
WAS OF THE CLOSEST
and only brought to an end by the voice that boomed 'COME!'
on the banks of the Shatt al Bilharz a dozen years ago now.
He never spoke less than highly of my *oeuvre*
and indeed would abjure me never to accept
less than twenty for a poem, so I think it would be a pity
if the fact that I temporarily haven't got any
were to be used as an excuse
to exclude me from this *Festschrift*.

If I could have finished the other thing
then I know you would have admired the way I dealt
with the need I feel to envisage familiar farms
as tenurial units which continue to sprawl on the land
during midnight downpours even when I'm not present,
but I couldn't, so there's no point continuing in this vein
and upsetting myself with thoughts of the postal order for a
fairly substantial sum which I'm certain you would have agreed
with me that it merited.

ANYWAY,

let me know soon what you think of my simple proposal,
hasten to be assured of the importance I have always attached
to my association with your excellent magazine,
and should you see Jaroslaw please stress quite forcibly to him
that the next time he uses one of my lines without
acknowledgement he'll be liable to find
that dawn is not the only thing that goes off like a gun,
the implication being that guns *sensu stricto*
have also been known to act in this way on occasion.

I await your reply with fervent anticipation
and in the meantime, Sir, have the honour to remain,
as ever, and as indigently, one who must be accounted
the foremost among your admirers, namely

The Cartoon Version

Two o'clock again, and the afternoon rains begin.
The longest wet summer of my getting much longer life
runs *amok* on the roof of the shack in which I work,
a long low unit stranded in the claylands,
where archaeologists get what they deserve
and the County Council pastures its yellow snow-ploughs.
The fertile *ennui* of this pottery researcher
knows no bounds on a Thursday afternoon,
and nor does the glistening god in a *sarong*
who leans from the crown of his swaying palm tree
to peer through my, to him, translucent roof
at these tables laid out with broken potsherds galore.
'Ee,' he says, 'Ah can allus tell
when *tha*'s been doin' t'bloody washin' up,'
then flies back to his jungle heaven and his girls,
to recite an elegant Sanskrit stanza about me
and enjoy their giggling disbelief at his tales.

The Coffin Factory

(for James Booth)

I work next door to a coffin factory.
Offcuts of veneer get blown from its yard
by playful zephyrs, then proceed to slither around
in the gutters and dusty grass
of our semi-industrial suburb.
Only last week, a two-metre strip of the stuff
molested my ankles on the bridge across the canal
so that suddenly I found myself engaging
in a curious ritual bound, a hero-leap,
to arrive on the other side of the stream
in a shower of grits and small gravels.
Lots of things offer to help me narrate this event
(dogs, serpents, land-adapted conger eels and so on)
but I'm tempted most to employ those dragon-banners
which Ammianus describes as having been borne
by the household troops of the Emperor Constantius
when he made his vicennial advent into Rome.
Their gaping mouths were so constructed, he tells,
as to hiss and roar in the breeze occasioned
by each horse's forward momentum, *so I can't help thinking*
that if some of them had escaped from their jewelled shafts
and gained the ground that day, learning to live and breed there
and become a part of the European fauna,
then it might well have been one of their offspring that attacked me,
sixteen hundred years later,
just beyond the gates of the coffin factory.

The Bear (The Sofas)

There was once a bear who longed to be a sofa.

The fact that he wasn't had caused him untold *angst*.

The ultimate day of his lonely life, however,
saw him find himself in a place among some rocks.

It was a natural amphitheatre, an Olympian court
on the razor-sharp circumference of which
a solemn council of *Achieved Furniture Bears*
was perched in down-gazing silence.

It was a cornucopia.

Grapes depended from vines,
which attempted to strangle branches;
honey dripped from the mouths of cool stone jars,
which unseen folk had wedged in the forks of elm trees;
ants as proud and muscle-bound as roosters
ran willy-nilly about the floor of the pit,
to consemble their *braggadocio* with the dawn.

He was overjoyed, this bear who longed to be sat upon.

'I'm about to become a Chesterfield,' he bellowed,
a piety which, untrue as it almost immediately transpired,
the fierce crags in their resolute sympathy
would bruit for a thousand years, *diminuendo*.

The Devil on Holiday

(for Jules Smith)

Satan gets the day off.
And go home early this afternoon as well, says the Boss.
See the world. Walk about in the sun.
I can manage on my own. *Besides, you deserve it.*

Satan doesn't argue. He's been tired, lately.
He feels like a worn-out guy in his middle forties,
in 1940s America, maybe on an August day
of immoderate humour, a single thud from the solar hammer
on a city whose sidewalks, underneath the hoof,
are of preternatural width and adamantine hardness,
and yea this city is the capital of a Beef State,
or it lies like a rock too big to be moved from a field.

OK Boss, says Satan. He is a worn-out old newshound,
and to this kind of news you can only respond with OKs,
so he takes his grey face, his grey trilby, and his
slab-like Robert Mitchum *Weltschmerz* and hooded eyes
out through the outer doors of *Pan Galactic Fantasy Comics Inc.*,
past the iced water and down to the burning street.

                              Is there a place called Duluth?

Or was there, maybe? Or shall there yet be one?

Satan doesn't know. He's never been to America,
has only the vaguest idea which planet it's on,
so he doesn't reply to himself, just knits his brows
as the trillion always accessible bites of data
begin to buzz like the flies he is held to be Lord of,
and there builds in his skull yet another consuming *Gestalt*.

So much for Intro. *You deserve no less.*
But meanwhile Satan is walking home
on that necklace of palm-fringed plazas which here in Duluth
is draped round the throat of the harbour, and we hurry to
            catch him up.

Which will not, as it happens, be difficult,
for Satan has stopped to think, and what he is thinking is
Shit, man, his apartment's in Sant' Angelo,
up on The Heights, not down here in Little Cuba
where even the fuckin' *Don't Walk* signs smell of cod
and for fuckssake how can he be so fuckin' stupid
as to've taken a left on Ninth instead of a right on Firestone?

Well, only Satan and one other Ineffably Plastic Entity
might care to answer that one, reader, but what you and I
are inexorably *into* is knowing what happens next,
not waiting for some bejewelled turtle
which swims in the World Ocean
and surfaces only once every million years
to come up with its head through the hole
of the plastic toilet seat which also apparently
floats about on said Ocean, so what I suggest is this,
speaking to Satan now, let us skip over
your bitter little self-deprecations
and catch you up in the gym.

Right. Fernando's Gym.

       Five floors up in a brownstone on Sweet Street.

Punchbag. Wallbars. Horse. Ring that reminds the visitor
of one of those white-fenced graveyards out on the prairie,
kind you got put in if you died on a wagon train.
Temple of manly arts. Sanctum of sweat and jock-itch.
Not really Satan's preferred kind of *locus.*

       Except for one thing.

It is cool.

Surprising as this information might seem, it is true.
It is the coolest gym in Duluth. The coolest place
that Satan has never been to. For present purposes,
it is the coolest place of all.

We deserve this, Satan. Yes.
And what we shall do to enjoy our well-deserved coolth
is first to bless the mishap and wrong left taken
which brought us to this den; second, to complete,
before mounting of stairs is over
the donning of The Discreetly Invisible Cloak;
and third, just to make sure,
send Morpheus the sleepy slave before us,
by breathing upon to entomb the inhabitants' eyes.

It is done.
Satan can stand in the door of the exercise hall
without fear of recognition. He casts about.
All men. Fernando himself, it must be,
towel round his neck. A white Caucasian baker,
doing a bootlace up. Black guy asleep on a broom.
Thank goodness for that.
No need to take his bifurcated cock
(in two of his hands to wank)
need be felt on this occasion.
Things are looking up. All he has to do
is bask in low temperatures, stroll around
in a comfy realm that is Heaven, compared to Duluth,
explore the john,
and enjoy himself until he begins to get bored.

And yet.
        Already something is wrong.

Satan, still invisible, grows immense inside his wrath.

Fernando turns into a puddle,
the baker a last week's copy of *The West Duluth Encounter*,
the sweeper a baby again, crawling about on the floor.

PANG. *It is not deserved.* PANG, PANG...

Satanic Majesty sweeps to the farthest reach
of the now explicably charred but still chilly gymnasium
and looks out through the fire-escape door, ajar,
right into the furnace that is the sky above Duluth.

PANG.
A kid in a wheelchair, maybe Fernando's boy,
has been parked on the edge of the rusty aerial platform
and is shooting steel balls at a can on the much lower roof
of the building across the street. Satan's eyes narrow.
He imagines becoming a fly of such dark size and weight
that by lifting the bright red brake at the back
of the boy's old-fashioned chair he'll cause a propulsive arc
that will end in a shower of edible snails on the sidewalk,
maybe make the papers.
He becomes this fly.

And now something incredible happens.

Instead of launching the child without delay
he decides a look at the face will be in order
so projects himself slowly down the kid's line of sight,
but a little above it,
thirty yards before dropping and starting to turn.

The boy is blind, as well. The bloated king of the *Diptera*
is aware of this even as he holds the burning air, spins,
and begins to come back up the flight path to the gantry.

So how can the kid take aim? Satan stops in mid-air.

I manage OK I guess.

It's as if the kid
is speaking inside his head, without permission,
in a voice he handles lazily, as one might a cattle-prod.
Satan stares at him. He feels tired.
He seems to be walking inside a blue steel tube
in phosphorescent light, going somewhere,
towards an infant at play by the side of a pool,
a tableau that gets repeated again and again,
so that each time Satan passes overhead the same things recur,
the baby disappears and the pool has become
a sodden page of newsprint, ENJOY
in six-inch headlines of the banner variety
YOUR SUMMER IN DULUTH.

When Satan re-assembles, he is walking north on Firestone.
Feeling good. Organising a complex beat
from the rhythms of two of his hearts. Jiving.
He isn't accustomed to feeling this kind of good.
It must be what happens when you find you've done the right thing.
Not like him to allow himself to be gooked
in the multi-faceted eye, *No Sir!*, the giving of treats
a little out of character perhaps,
but then sometimes enough is enough, destruction, mayhem,
especially that black guy... baby rather...
Satan starts to laugh,
and laughing makes him feel so good that he brings a *third* heart in,
and now an intricate music makes flowers fall from the sky:
tulips, roses, foxgloves, colombines, carnations,
daisies, bugloss, borage, many little blue stars.
And then a fourth. The sidewalk looks like a Persian carpet
or the scene of an outrage inside an eclectic florist's.
Satan looks up. A guy who smells a bit like freshly baked bread
has just stepped out of a doorway, cap in one hand,
wiping his gleaming brow with the back of the other
and asking Satan
what he makes of all these preposterous flowers, Mac?
Satan considers his answer. The guy thinks, Jesus,
I'd like to punch this bastard on the nose,
and I don't know why,
but he takes a single step forwards, just the same.

Satan looks at him. There plays on his face the most courteous
          of smiles.

I'm on holiday, he says. *Besides, the kid deserved it.*

On Crete or Somewhere

(for Sam Milne)

The peasant here, before the Second World War,
was wont to reckon the distance between ravines
in terms of the number of acrid cigarettes
he would need upon the journey.

To the edge of that darkness a score.
The outcrop yonder then nine.
Thousand on thousand my friend.

He used to move through upland fields of stone
on the back of donkey or mule; it was often winter;
his saturnine and unrelenting ways
were marked by chains of smoke in the lifeless air,
entwined with those left by brigands, gendarmes,
priests who buttoned their beards beneath their coats.

Sitting Propped Up in the Side-Galleries

Once they were adventurers who dared
to come in search of the glittering fruits of the earth.

Now the most they can do is tumble apart
to frighten girls in crotch-hugging dun-coloured shorts.

God in Heaven, the way their jaws clack open!
The way they offer bone's best to the mirage of flesh!

Individual Culture

I

The oven gloves were not to hand,
so I picked up the kettle
with a pink sponge rabbit, which was.

II

The rain arranges round every oak tree's bole
splashes like the gaping mouths of nestlings.

III

You tried to get your favourite private word
admitted into the Oxford English Dictionary,
but they weren't having any,
and so you continue to *groblitz* only with friends.

IV

If wine were blue there would be no need
to describe this singular sky.

V

Above the faceless heads of the crowd
a tuba seems to be gulping light from the snow,
trying to rid its mouth of the taste of warplanes.

Common Property

I'm lying of course
but I once had a morse telegraphist friend
who told me how startled he'd been one rainy evening
to hear the upturned bucket in his yard
instruct him quaintly to go and eat his mother.

I revealed in return how obsessed I'd become
with the notion of raindrops falling inside the chimney,
adding to thousands of feet through clandestine air
another thirty through the centre of my house.

The Seventeenth of June
(for Ken Steedman)

Back at tea-time. And a lace-wing inside the house.
Lovely *Chrysopa*, on a towel smelling of rain.
Which shews patience enough to bask a while in our joy
(at its having been rescued from death by folding up)
then disappears at speed about its business.
I think I will thank Saint Briavel for this,
whose day it is,
and about whose life nothing, whatsoever, is known.

I encountered a fellow pluviophile earlier on.
The sudden secret handshake of our talk
I must confess has cheered me up no end.
There it incredibly was,
the telling me how in weather akin to this,
his wife would opine him crazy,
his fancy to sleep among lumber in the shed.
Pass friend; and when you cease to exist
go straight to Heaven, up through a summer downpour,
but keeping dry all the while, as if there had never
been other ways to travel.

The day recounts itself backwards.
At the bus stop this morning
I was thinking how simple it sometimes actually is
just to set things in motion,
to do as we've every One been done by, in fact.
I hoped that when the evening finally came, as it has,
I might find some words about English coastal parishes,
each with its beacon, spire, gallows,
ragstone tower or en-hillocked elm as landfall,
to be battered towards by crumster, cog and barque
through stillicidous arras or wrist-wraithing bone-racking sea-roke.
And here they are.
I wasn't quite sure what I wanted them for at the time
but now, in this silence, I bless their superfluity,
welling over the rounded rim of a day
of huge balneation, spargefaction wide,
the workings of grace made both pertinent and strange,
its conduits quick with all the sanctions of water.

Line with Atoll and Idol

As if were being drawn a thin black line
in the air a dozen feet above the sea.

As if it travelled parallel with Ocean,
but Ocean lay calm in an everywhere shallow bed,
devoid of ornament,
and never did wave snap hungrily up at the sky.

And as if that part of the line which moved
(for always these things are hard to comprehend)
made headway toward a coast,

but the bench of the island beach
sat nearly a dozen yards above the water,

and the line in its blackness was halted.

And as if, held in a nimbus of black sand,
the glassy basalt pillbox of the island
were nodding like a head from the eighteenth century,
which wore in accordance
with fashions not now understood by us,
two cloths as caps, the first argillaceous
                    and the second a yellowing sward.

And centred on this atoll were sitting astride
the ridge-pole of her roof a Golden Woman,
who laughed, and cried, and sang, and through whom, waving,
expressed itself a continuum of frenzy;

and as if the thing most worthy to be noted
were how, if she'd only known that she existed,
she'd have ruled her *Realm Entire* from that vantage,
scanned the lagoon,
tasted the brassy sun as a serpent
lying coiled upon her shoulder,
and the rain in the wise of the forest's waxen cups;

and as if this were true, and All, and she marked from her chair
on its special swivelling mount
the four tracks which, when they met in the slits of her eyes,
had quartered the island between them, and made into a temple
her house through the doorless apertures of which,
in search of its earthen floor, the fowl from the woods
had all day strutted and pecked, and her eyes were not figments,
and the island more than smoke on the distant horizon,
and the thin black line which had travelled so far over Ocean
with its beach-head secure were now moving inland from the shore.

Cosmological

Spirals of brick-red gas.
Mind that broods
on the interstellar wind.
Sign of the Gnostic Heart of Jesus Christ,
creaking and swaying outside some deep-space tavern.

And here we stand.
Staring into the farthest reaches of cold.
A dog bays at the moon,
and that ever dutiful engine
hears and hurls the Holy Family's shadow
to be splintered against the earth,
to be thieves caught climbing among the star-blanched boulders
which strew our hillsides,
beneath the walls of our towns.

Staff Only

I'm drinking tea in a furniture store,
idly thinking of Phoebus, the sun-god,
when a sky-blue sofa on which a youth reclines
glides slowly through the cafeteria,
pulled by a couple of girls in nylon shop-coats.

I used to enjoy such theological problems
but now they make me tired, as one is tired by a child.

I watch in the last few minutes of my lunch-hour
this tableau as it steers its direct course
towards regions where no customer ever goes,
through swinging doors equipped with rubber aprons
which gasp behind it as it disappears from view.

Pokerwork

I fell in love with the vine-entangled cabin
in the instant of reading its charmingly different name.

The fact that I'd rented the only shack
on the whole damn mountain
that wasn't called *Cloudy Pines*,
White Smoke Table,
or *Iron Moon-Kettle Madly Boiling Over*,
didn't perturb me at all.

I knew as soon as I set down my bags at the gate
that if there was one kind of conversation
I certainly wouldn't be overhearing that summer
as friends made plans outside the General Store
while I purchased kerosene
in its cool, high-raftered and oatmeal-scented interior
it was this:

'How about taking some beer and climbing up
to *Bucket of Rusty Nuts and Bolts* this evening?
Watch the stars rise. Have us a *haiku* party.'

No. I think I can fairly claim that right from the start
I'd have wagered the end-most joint of one of my fingers,
to be severed against a boulder if I lost,
that this was not what the Boundless Void was proposing.

Not that I minded. As I say,
I loved my chalet from the moment I first saw
its cedarwood signboard,
the deeply scorched and somehow rococo calligraphy of which
inspired me with wonder, longing, and most deeply reverenced
presentiments of solitude.

An Office Memo

TO: *Julia*
FROM: *Brian*

When I got here first thing this morning
I discovered Gabriel, that trainee you sent us,
kneeling down as if composed for prayer
in front of my micro-computer.
I registered my surprise,
whereon he quite brusquely gave me to understand
how certain he was he could put it together again.
He called me 'Jack', and exhorted me not to panic.
I would probably not lose many, if any,
of my files. There were numerous yellow 'bobbin'
things lying beside him, carefully arranged
in the form of a Cross of Lorraine.
These he proposed to 'de-coke', I think he said,
with judiciously moistened twists of toilet paper.
I found his nonchalant, 'make-do-and-mend',
supremely proletarian kind of self-confidence
quite distasteful, and must have telegraphed as much,
for he stamped on my foot and proceeded to disappear.
I feel poorly, and am just about to go home.
The bobbins have begun to tick and smoke.
I thought I had better
get in touch with you about this.

The Tar on the Roads

Seventh day of the heat wave.
Buying fags after work I tried to remember
the last time the tar on the roads had melted.
She said with cars going past all afternoon
it had sounded as if it were raining.

There was quite a queue at the bus stop.
The man standing next to me said it needed a shelter.
Before the winter came.
I said I knew what a very grim place it was
to find oneself on a January evening.

When the bus arrived, I paid and went upstairs.
All one side was old people, coming back from the coast.
They looked really done in.
They sat alone on the outside of their seats,
and guarded the empty spaces next to them.
It meant I couldn't get myself by a window
on the left of the bus, as I like to,
and consequently had to sit down on the right.

I was faintly annoyed.
And desperately hot.
And rather keenly looking forward
to discussing the heat with my wife,
to telling her all about loudly hissing tar.
As far as I recall,
no one spoke in that upper saloon
during the whole half-hour of my journey.
I stared from my window.
I watched someone close a window against a draught.
I looked at the yellow fields of the valley floor,
and once I let myself glance across the aisle
at the faces of the pensioners,
but they seemed so tired and angry
that I chose not to do so again.

I was glad when the time came to walk.

The pavements were empty
and the melting road had been dusted with fine white gravel
so that everything looked like a postcard of nineteen-thirteen.

I was very hot indeed.

The worst thing I ever heard on that bus
came out of the mouth of a soldier going on leave
from the Army Transport School,
a mouth he was using to tell another squaddie
of what he'd always wanted to do to old women,
pointing one out down below as we crawled in the traffic,
walking beside us with some letters in her hand.

That was on a summer afternoon too,
one not as hot as this, and when I finally got in the house
the living room was like an oven, and my wife and I turned
each a gasping visage upon the other.
The television was going
and the newsreader was saying to several million people
that Highways Departments throughout the entire region
had been forced to grit the roads today to stop
the tar on them melting, except she didn't call it tar,
having had her orders to refer to it as bitumen.

He Loves to Go A-Wandering

Alone on an upland trail,
having left his wristwatch at home,
he takes a telescope out
and scans the surrounding hills.

What luck!
There's a long-case clock in a meadow of wind and herbs
with its face turned towards him,
and it's not as late as he thought.

He observes it long enough to make sure
that the minute hand *is* moving
then stows the glass
and continues on his way.

Later, towards evening,
with a limestone boulder serving as rustic desk,
he lays out notebook, bacon beer and pencil,
and memorialises thus:

The Lord is my Shepherd.
Special pockets all I hoped they would be.
Telescope splendid for telling time among mountains.

A Malediction

Spawn of a profligate hog.
May the hand of your self-abuse
be afflicted by a palsy.
May an Order in Council
deprive you of a testicle.
May your teeth be rubbed with turds
by a faceless thing from Grimsby.
May your past begin to remind you
of an ancient butter paper
found lying behind a fridge.
May the evil odour of an elderly male camel
fed since birth on buckets of egg mayonnaise
enter your garden and shrivel up all your plants.
May all reflective surfaces
henceforth teach you to shudder.
And may you thus be deprived
of the pleasures of walking by water.
And may you grow even fatter.
And may you, moreover, develop athlete's foot.
May your friends cease to excuse you,
your wife augment the thicket of horns on your brow,
and even your enemies weary of malediction.
May your girth already gross
embark on a final exponential increase.
And at the last may your body, in bursting,
make your name live for ever,
an unparalleled warning to children.

A Bee

Become at last a bee
I took myself naked to town,
with plastic sacks of yellow turmeric
taped to my wizened thighs.

I'd been buying it for weeks,
along with foods I no longer had a need for,
in small amounts from every corner grocer,
so as not to arouse their suspicion.

It was hard, running and buzzing,
doing the bee-dance. I ached
at the roots of my wings, and hardly yet discerned
that I flew towards reparation,
that in my beehood my healing had been commenced.

Words they use in this hive. To me it seems still
that clumps of tall blue flowers,
which smiled as they encroached,
had been born of my apian will,
in which to my shame I struggled for a moment,
and stained the air with clouds of my dearly bought gold.

Next

Next is a porcelain plaque,
fixed by a nail
to the trunk of a churchyard yew.
There's a supercilious pillock in a trenchcoat
standing next to it, holding a clipboard,
and talking straight to camera.
Yeah, right first time.
It wouldn't surprise me
if he's talking about that plaque,
but then again
his subject might be anything.
Putting him under the tree,
in its ravaged circle of acid litter and gloom,
might prove to have been a mistake, though,
for now the rain-cleansed afternoon country
which falls away in all directions behind him,
will come out wrongly exposed.
This may, of course, be the very effect they're after.
Or it may be they just don't care.
The plaque carried an inscription once,
a biblical reference
in black and heavily serifed Roman caps
which nowadays is eloquent only
of the sad effects of two hundred years of weather.
I love that kind of thing.
You can still read the name of the Book in question (*Judges*),
but chapter and verse have completely eroded away.

Jottings from Northern Minsters

I

limestone jazz

woodland clearing
with stiff-leaved clarinet

doorthud on airspace
where echoes fall into dust

for regimental colours
a row of smoking trombones

II

Cathedral Shadow
flits the length of the nave.

Squats on the altar rail
staring into the light.

I think he's recalling
his life as M.R. James.

I hear him implore me
to change him back to a sparrow.

III

Lightning at York,
to many in the Faith,
was a sure and certain sign of Divine displeasure
at the blasphemous enthronement
of Jenkins as Bishop of Durham.

I don't see it that way.

If God had really deployed Omnipotent Fire
it would doubtless have been for more amusing reasons,
perhaps to alleviate local unemployment
with a nicely considered Job Creation Scheme.

IV

The poet staggers down to the end of his garden.
Directs a stream of piss at a clump of bluebells.
Completely bloody useless.
He's wasting his time
with this stuff about cathedrals.
He gazes at his shoes.
And quite without warning
discovers the night transformed into *Oberon's Glade*.
He raises his head. Above the rooftops
a wind from the south has shoved some clouds aside
and the lunar chalice is spilling its silver light
through the delicate tracery
of his neighbour's mountain ash.
It takes a moment, then the poet starts to laugh.
A state of gleeful reverence sets in.
All the way back to the house he sniggers and nurtures
the penultimate grace of knowing he'll finish the poem.

An Expedition

Down to the end of the garden in the night.
With cigarette and glass of ice-cold milk.
I pick my way over heaps of builders' rubble.
Light from the new kitchen window comes along too.

Spade
(for Sarah)

Spade that wedges
the broken door of the hutch
and stops our rabbit
escaping into the night

Spade which denies to black rabbit
his leaping over the sage
his crouching in warm dark wind
his vanishing act until morning

Spade which gets handed
like a baton by moon to sun
and has been with me years, houses

Spade that but a moment ago
I imagined made out of glass

Sunday

(for Pat)

You start to wash the window,
find yourself peering out
at a foggy autumn morning.
Then you stop and smile.
Just can't tell
if you're getting it clean or not.
When you've gone
I sit and stare at the fence
where it joins the back of the house.
It's all I can see.
A sparrow lands on it,
but only for a moment –
the length of time it takes
to leave it empty again.

Elegiac Alternatives

I

Along the hull of an unladen barge,
riding high in the yellow afternoon,
the river casts reflections that resemble
the distant wingspans of ocean-going birds,
glimpsed at the moment of their sudden coalescence
into one great pensive Form,
beating low above shining level waters,
in certain flight towards an unseen coast.

II

Rabbits graze the edge of a cornfield at dusk.
A wicker bath-chair hangs in the top of a tree,
the roots of which hang over the edge of a chalk-pit,
its floor already in shadow. Another night begins.
Flame goes aloft in the rigging of the thorn
to view the sun as it sinks below the hill.
In the aftermath of an almost forgotten explosion
unspent appetite poses a moment as silence.

Chandlery

Here is your wooden keg.

It contains your astrolabe,
carefully packed in oysters.

I could do you black powder
if you cared to change your mind.

Or from perfect darkness a tethered animal,
one that would give you some milk.

One Mile Wide

Way it gets dark here.
Down by the water
the sky turns out its pockets
and goes to sleep in the grass.
Five white stones next morning.
All night long the river singing of home
to stones which might
if things had not been different
have been stars.